alamosa

The San Luis Valley's Big City

by

LELAND FEITZ

Introduction
by

ALEX J. CHAVEZ

Published by
LITTLE LONDON PRESS
716 E. Washington St.
Colorado Springs, Colorado

Library of Congress
Card Number 76-3899

INTRODUCTION

As I read this historical sketch of Alamosa and the San Luis Valley, many memories flash by of childhood on a farm near La Jara, not many miles from the Feitz farm and about twenty miles from Alamosa. This sketch also brings to mind many pleasant memories of close friends — friends with whom both Leland and I identified: the Ujiharas; the Newcombs; the Roybals; the Yoshidas; the Stamps, and others, of course. We all attended La Jara High School and graduated, in 1942, in a class numbering nineteen!

I have read, with interest, the historical Booklets that Leland Feitz has written about other places in Colorado. This same desire to preserve the past has also led me to collect, record, and perform the folk music of the Hispano of Southern Colorado and Northern New Mexico.

It is this common interest; our many years as classmates, and our friendship that makes me feel proud and honored to have been asked to write the first page of this book!

Alex J. Chavez
Assistant Professor of Music
Adams State College

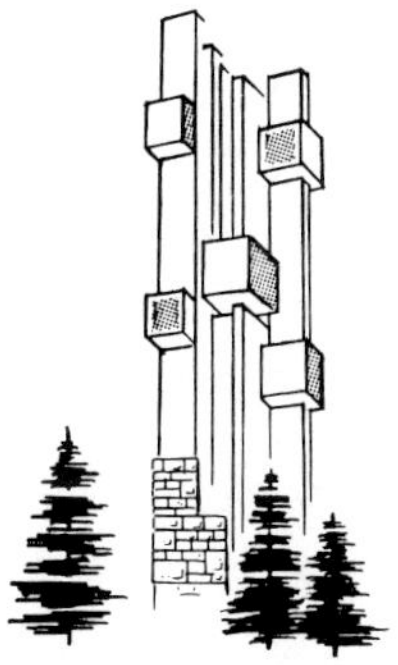

LELAND FEITZ

The author was born in La Jara, Colorado and spent the first eighteen years of his life in the San Luis Valley. Moving to Colorado Springs to attend Colorado College, Feitz then followed a career in advertising and public relations.

An ardent history buff, Feitz began writing and publishing concise history booklets about Colorado people and places in 1967. His Little London Press, established in 1973, has now published over twenty Colorado history booklets with a combined circulation of over 150,000.

In addition to operating his own publishing business, Feitz serves as Publications Director for Century One Press of Colorado Springs, a major producer of Western Americana.

Even though Feitz now lives in Colorado Springs and Cripple Creek, his interests are still centered in the San Luis Valley as evidenced by his booklets about Alamosa, Creede, Platoro, and feature stories in the *Pueblo Star Journal & Chieftain* focusing on people of the valley.

TABLE OF CONTENTS

Alexander Cameron Hunt, founder of the city of Alamosa. Before he became associated with General William Jackson Palmer in building the Denver & Rio Grande Railroad, Hunt had been Governor of the Colorado Territory. Hunt is buried in the Congressional Cemetery in Washington. (Western History Department, Denver Public Library)

Alamosa's water tower has been a landmark for half a century. The city's pure water comes from six deep wells. Buildings of the Public Service Company can be seen at the right.

FOREWORD

Alamosa! I love the sound of the name and I love the city itself. It will always be a very special place to me. This feeling I have for it stems from a happy childhood, when just about everything exciting in my young life centered around the San Luis Valley's big town. To a boy growing up during the depression on a farm outside a town of some 500 souls, a city of 5,000 seemed immense and filled with wonders. Then nothing could match the thrill of a trip to Gordon's Department Store, the Rialto Theatre, or the Grand Cafe!

Almost every Saturday during my early years my mother and I loaded up our '29 Chevy with a dozen or so pounds of fresh butter and a case of eggs and headed up the road to Alamosa to "trade." Farm people didn't shop for groceries in those days. We "traded." Our good farm produce was swapped for coffee, tea, sugar, and the few things we couldn't grow on our La Jara farm. If mother got as much as 20c a pound for her butter and 10c for a dozen eggs she felt pretty good.

Sometimes there would be a few cents left from the exchange and we'd splurge and eat out. Hamburgers were six for a quarter at the Alamo Lunch. Or, if we felt a little ritzy, we'd *dine* on chop suey at the Shanghai or Grand. Alamosa's cafes and stores were crowded with other farm families every Saturday, so the whole day turned into something of a big social blast.

Alamosa was always at its very best during the summer months when the vegetable harvest was in full swing and a little more money stirred. Then a string of wonderful attractions found their way to our isolated valley.

One of the big ones was the Alamo Exposition Shows. It was a giant of a carnival that turned an east Alamosa riverside lot into a regular Coney Island for a week. My folks usually rounded up a bunch of kids my age and took us up for opening night. Sometimes I had as much as $1.00 to spend on the games, shows, and rides. We'd mill around the midway until midnight when the carnival's big free show took place. At no other time of the year were we ever up that late.

The summer attraction we looked forward to most was the annual appearance of Fred G. Brunk's Comedians. A tent show, Brunk's played Alamosa for one full week each summer with a different play each night and a special matinee on Saturday. While there were no Richard Burtons traveling with Brunk's, their plays and their players were good, we thought, and it was our only touch with live theatre.

Cole Brothers, Al G. Barnes, and Hagenbeck-Wallace were a few of the big circuses to pitch their bigtops in the alkali fields just south of town. When the family budget didn't allow for the price of tickets, which was often the case, we'd drive up to Alamosa early in the morning to see the circus train arrive and unload. Then we'd follow their bright wagons to the circus grounds and watch the whole wonderful thing take shape. Sometimes there would be a parade up Main Street. Missing the show itself didn't seem too bad after spending a whole day in the city watching the frenzy of activity around the circus lot.

When Fall came, if there had been a decent potato crop and if there had been a market for them, we'd hit Alamosa in high spirits and in a buying mood. That was the time of the year we generally spruced up our wardrobes. Mother loved the quality of the stuff the Leon Sisters carried, but their prices were a little higher than those at the Classic Shop or Gordon's. It was only when she could find a dress or coat that was greatly reduced that she would come home with a Leon Sister's label. Dad's clothes came from the men's department at Gordon's. And they came darn seldom. He just never could see any reason to buy a suit when he had a suit. I loved the mad jumble of merchandise piled around in Bain's big store, and that is where most of my school clothes came from.

Once a year, after mother sold her turkey crop, the Feitz's launched a really big scale shopping attack on Alamosa. The turkey crop was her one big source of income each year, and whether or not the taxes or the Federal Land Bank had been paid, this was *her* money. Coming a little before Christmas, most of it went for presents, But she usually held out enough to buy something new for our home — a chair from Kirkpatrick's, a set of dishes from Ward's, a little piece of silver from Velhaugen's.

Only a trip to the Rialto Theatre for a Sunday matinee beat the fun of spending the "turkey money." The Rialto is where we celebrated birthdays, holidays, and anniversaries. Dad could never quite understand why mother and I made him drive fifteen miles to and from Alamosa to see a show for 45c we could see in La Jara in a few months for 25c. But he went along with it anyway and sometimes took us up early enough so we could go to one of the city's fancy churches.

Some of our Alamosa trips were in the interest of our health. The best doctors and dentists in the valley were there. So Alamosa is where we went to get our tonsils out and our teeth cleaned. Most people of the valley who became seriously sick ended up at the big white ether-smelling hospital on Main Street.

Alamosa is where we went to get our prescriptions filled, our clothes cleaned, and our car greased. That's where we bought insurance, borrowed money, and sought legal advice. We danced at the Elk's Club, skated at the Coconut Grove, and sipped sodas at Sherm's. Alamosa is where we went to get our hair cut and our pictures taken. It was the place to go for ball games, band concerts, and Farm Bureau meetings. Alamosa was the place to trade cars, buy furniture, and get a watch fixed. We read the *Alamosa Courier* and listened to KGIW. We heard about all the wild women over on Front Street and the all night poker games at the Victoria Hotel, and we knew quite a bit about the community's leading bootlegger. We admired the big school buildings and fine churches, used the Carnegie Library, and bragged about how my sister had been one of the first students to enroll at Adams State Normal School. We were proud when Billy Adams spoke to us and we admired Mayor Cole. We thought Joe Brite was the greatest theatre organist in the world. Alamosa was the place you went to catch a bus or meet a train. It's where you bought decorated birthday cakes and flowers for funerals. In Alamosa you could learn to play bridge, sing, and tap dance. And, God knows, you could come close to freezing to death!

Now, I have been away from the San Luis Valley for some thirty years. Having seen some of the world's great cities in the meantime, I find Alamosa doesn't look quite as big or seem quite as bright as it did when I went there to talk to Santa Claus. But because it was the first city in my life, I expect it will always be my special favorite.

Leland Feitz

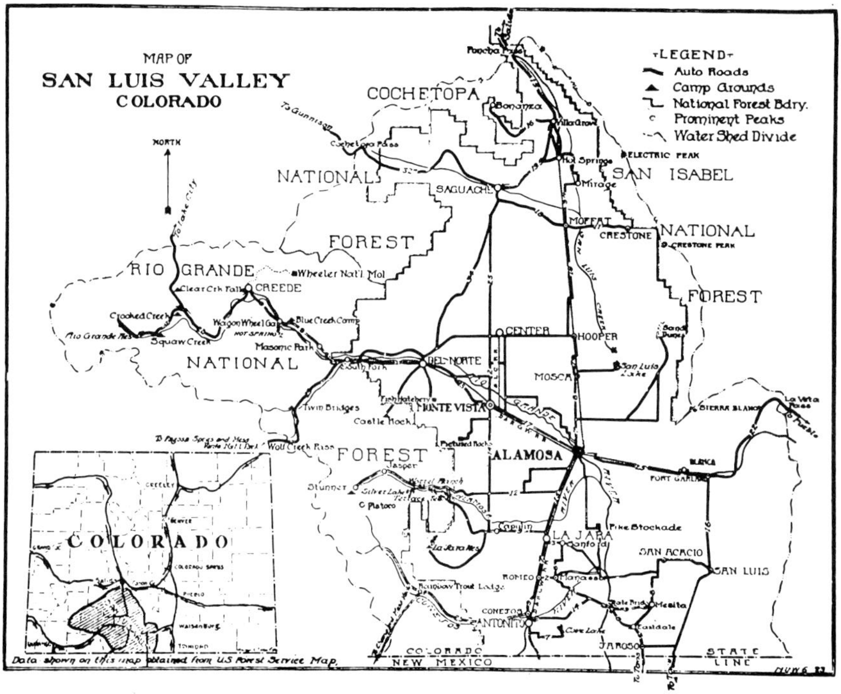

MAP OF
SAN LUIS VALLEY
COLORADO

LEGEND
Auto Roads
Camp Grounds
National Forest Bdry.
Prominent Peaks
Water Shed Divide

Data shown on this map obtained from U.S. Forest Service Map.

The San Luis Valley occupies an area about the size of the state of Connecticut in south-central Colorado.

Alamosa is surrounded by sensational scenery. The Great Sand Dunes and the Sangre de Cristo Mountains are just to the north of the city.

A LITTLE ABOUT THE LOCATION

Sometimes chambers of commerce are given to exaggeration when it comes to selling the world on their communities' features. That's not so with the one in Alamosa. They simply call it "A Wonderful Place to Live," and that is a quiet understatement.

While the long, cold winters may be something of a drawback, that's about all that can be found wrong with the place. It does get cold as anyone who listens to weather reports knows. Alamosa is often the nation's coldest spot. Once the temperature dipped to fifty below.

But Alamosa's frigid setting is absolutely magnificent! The city sits at an elevation of 7,540 feet on a bend of the Rio Grande River right in the middle of the great San Luis Valley in south-central Colorado. Actually a high mountain park, the valley is about the size of the state of Connecticut. It is surrounded by some of the most spectacular mountains in America, and some of the highest.

Quiet rivers with lovely Spanish names meander through ranch and farm lands. Wildlife abounds. The sun shines just about every day of the year. Pollution is unheard of, the air is crystal clear, and the sky is about as blue as the turquoise some of the foothills produce. The great white clouds seen over the valley are, somehow, more beautiful than clouds are any other place. And at sunrise and sunset the mountains turn pink and then purple in one of natures' great "spectaculars."

San Luis Valley pioneer and one-time resident of Alamosa, J. Heber Mott, claimed the valley couldn't be compared with any other spot on earth. He was right. The geography and vastness of the place defies description. There just aren't enough good adjectives.

Few places have a backdrop to equal Alamosa's! Sierra Blanca (elevation 14,345) one of America's most massively majestic mountains, towers over the town. This picture of the San Luis Valley's famous landmark was taken in 1935 by The Wilhelm's, noted Alamosa photographers.

These are some of the buildings hauled into Alamosa from old Garland City. The building on the corner in this 1880 photograph housed The Broadwell House. The buildings are facing Sixth Street west from Hunt. (State Historical Society of Colorado)

When Alamosa was very young, the commercial center faced the railroad tracks along Sixth Street between San Juan and Hunt. The "X" identifies the Perry House, one of the buildings brought into Alamosa from Garland City. It stood where the Victoria Hotel is now located. (State Historical Society of Colorado)

IN THE BEGINNING

One morning Alamosa didn't amount to much; that night it did. A lot of Colorado towns sprung up quick-like, but none grew quite like this one. It was platted, and then a train load of ready-made buildings were hauled in and put on the lots. The whole thing was engineered by the sharp people who built the Denver & Rio Grande Railroad.

The thrust of the Denver & Rio Grande toward the San Luis Valley began in 1876 as the rails reached La Veta. By the summer of 1877, a narrow gauge road had been built over La Veta Pass as far as the construction camp of Garland City, about six miles east of Fort Garland. The following summer, the road was completed to the bend of the Rio Grande where Alamosa was to be built. Earlier, when the great San Luis Valley was criss-crossed with stage routes, the bend in the river was one of the stops.

Alexander Cameron Hunt selected the location during the summer of 1877 as he was scouting the valley for town sites and rail routes. A close associate of General William Jackson Palmer, founder of the railroad, Hunt, at the time he founded Alamosa, was president of the Denver & Rio Grande Construction Co. Earlier, this "human whirlwind," as Palmer called him, had been governor of the Colorado Territory.

Feeling the location at the bend of the river would be a logical site for a city, Hunt wrote Palmer as follows after his visit to the spot in 1877:

> ". . . beyond La Veta Pass lands us in the very center of the most arable land to be found in Colorado or the whole Rocky Mountains, and when the facilities for irrigation are considered in all their bearings, I believe I can say with safety that no other locality with equal advantages can be found between the Gulf of Mexico and the British possessions. The spot where I have stopped the rails, as shown on the map of the country (enclosed) which spot is christened Rio Bravo is upon the southwest bank of the Rio Grande equidistant from the two ranges of mountains."

At the time Hunt wrote Palmer about the proposed townsite, access to it was by crossing the river on a rope ferry. Then, before any of the Rio Grande's water was used for irrigation, it was some 400 to 500 feet wide and deep enough that some effort was made toward steam navigation on it.

The new town's prospects for the future were bright from the time the railroad acquired Hunt's proposed site. Naming it Alamosa (Spanish for cottonwood), the plat was filed in May of 1878. Incorporation followed in August. Between the two dates, the rails came and Alamosa boomed.

Hill's, one of Alamosa's largest early general merchandise houses. Isaac Hill made a fortune supplying early land developers, ditch companies, and mine owners with supplies and machines. The big store stood beside the tracks, south of Sixth Street. (State Historical Society of Colorado)

The Elkhorn, an Alamosa "gentlemen's club" of the 1880's. It faced Sixth Street, once also called "Saloon Street," and for good reason. (State Historical Society of Colorado)

The narrow gauge road into the new town site was completed on June 22, and the first train brought flat cars loaded with an odd assortment of buildings from the deserted construction camp of Garland City. The "freight" included the Broadwell and Occidental Hotels and the Gem Saloon. Later, these were joined by the Perry House. On the day the Perry House made its thirty-mile move, proprietor Joe Perry pulled an inn-keeping feat without equal. That morning, he served his guests a big breakfast in Garland City; that night he served them supper in the same building in its new Alamosa location.

The Garland City buildings and most of the new ones to sprout up around them were located along the tracks facing the depot. What is now Sixth Street was the commercial center of the new town, with a few buildings scattered north on what would one day be Hunt and State.

With the further push of the railroad halted for a time, Alamosa grew as an outfitting point for all of southern Colorado and northern New Mexico. Large supply houses were built along the tracks and stocked with an assortment of goods for the ranches of the area and for the mines of the San Juan country. Enormous wagon trains arrived at the railhead loaded with ore and left town loaded with supplies for Lake City, Gunnison, and other communities not yet connected with the rest of the world by rails. There were daily stages to and from Lake City, Gunnison, Saguache, Pitkin, and the New Mexico towns of Taos, Tierra Amarillo, and Santa Fe.

By 1880, with a population of over 800, Alamosa was the largest and the liveliest town in southern Colorado. A rowdy, wide-open place, its streets were filled with an assortment of railroad construction huskies, miners, sheep herders, cow punchers, and gamblers. There was a considerable Spanish speaking population, for Conejos County, in which Alamosa was then located, had been settled by the Spanish in 1854.

The town saw many lynchings during the early years, with a large cottonwood tree by the river serving as a handy scaffold. From one of its limbs, in 1880, the body of a Mexican cattle rustler dangled all day, a warning to other would-be rustlers.

The coming of religion to the frontier town didn't seem to take too well. Even though Rev. Alex M. Darley established a First Presbyterian Church there before the railroad reached the place, its growth was a bit slow. A Rev. J. J. Gilchrist, in the valley to do mission work among the Mexican people, reported in 1881:

> ". . . from March to June of this year, though the town has fully 1000 people, there was not a single sermon preached here."

A week after Gilchrist reached Alamosa, he conducted a burial out in the brush east of town. As they returned to the town his seat-mate, a saloon keeper, said: "Parson, we are so glad to have you here; we want someone to pray; it does not seem right to bury the dead without a word of prayer."

Gilchrist reported the church had only one member in 1881 — a woman who lived twenty miles from town. Two years later, the First Presbyterian Church boasted twenty members and by that time other denominations were starting to be active.

Except for its magnificent setting, almost at the foot of Mt. Blanca, Alamosa, with its assortment of hand-me-down buildings and deeply rutted streets, was sure no beauty spot. Because of its shifting population, it was not exactly an ideal spot to bring up a family. But all this was to change. With a good start Alamosa was destined for growth as the Denver & Rio Grande expanded in the valley.

COPYRIGHTED 1882 BY J. J. STONER, MADISON, WIS.

ALAMOSA, COLO.
1882

1 SCHOOL BUILDING
2 PRESBYTERIAN CHURCH
3 POST OFFICE
4 BANK OF SAN JUAN
5 PERRY HOUSE, NORMOYLE & BACHUS
6 BROADWELL HOUSE, D. P. BROADWELL
7 DEPOT
8 D & R G SHOPS
9 D & R G ROUND HOUSE
10 GREAT WESTERN STABLES, GEO. L. BLACKMORE

And that's the way it was in 1882! Originally all the east-west streets were given numbers, and north-south streets were simply lettered. State was first called G Street. When this sketch was made, the depot was one block east of where it is now, at the corner of Sixth and Hunt.

NARROW GAUGE RAILROAD CENTER

Because of political and financial problems in another part of the state, the Denver & Rio Grande's San Luis Valley expansion was halted until 1880. Then tracks were laid south, through La Jara, on to Antonito, and over Cumbres Pass to Chama, New Mexico. By 1881, Alamosa and Durango were connected by rails.

During the same period, construction was underway on the line south of Antonito which would eventually connnect it with Santa Fe. By the end of 1880, that road reached Espanola, New Mexico. But because of financial squabbles, it was seven long years before one of the Denver & Rio Grande's little trains ran all the way into Sante Fe.

While tracks were being laid to the south of Alamosa, other crews were busy pushing another road west through Monte Vista, Del Norte, and to South Fork. This construction was completed in 1881. Two years later, the road was extended up the scenic Rio Grande Canyon to Wagon Wheel Gap, where General Palmer built an elegant European-type spa for the well-heeled traveler. Wagon Wheel Gap remained the end of that branch only until 1891 when silver was discovered at Creede and the railroad was then extended to serve one of Colorado's greatest mining towns.

In the meantime, the Denver & Rio Grande was building a new line into the San Luis Valley from the north, first only from Salida to the very north end of the valley. The road was extended all the way into Alamosa in 1890.

By 1890, then, and for half a century to follow, Alamosa was the absolute center of narrow gauge railroading in America. The giant shops of the fourth division of the Denver and Rio Grande, built soon after Alamosa was founded, were expanded every year and hummed with day and night activity. From the busy depot, passenger trains arrived and departed daily for Denver, Durango, Santa Fe, Salida, and Creede.

Long freight trains arrived in Alamosa loaded with supplies for the developing valley; others left carrying ore, lumber, cattle, sheep, and farm products.

With prosperity assured and growth inevitable, the Denver & Rio Grande, in 1890, rebuilt the La Veta Pass road, making it standard gauge. Third rails were laid throughout the San Luis Valley so trains of both gauges could travel its broad expanse. The only three-track switching yards in the world were then built in Alamosa, and the giant shops were expanded once again.

It hadn't been planned that way, but for a time the Alamosa shops had something of a self-appointed mascot. A tramp dog, one winter, moved into the warm shop buildings and right into the hearts of the men who worked there. They named him "Boomer." Soon after his adoption into the Denver & Rio Grande family, Boomer started riding the trains with his new railroad friends. When he sensed a train was about to leave the Alamosa yards, he jumped into the little locomotive, taking a seat up front by the engineer as if he were a part of the crew.

While the arrival of the Denver & Rio Grande and its ten years of continuing expansion in the valley saw Alamosa grow from an idea to a lively town of about 1000 people, it was really the result of the railroad's being there that gave the place permanence and an on-going prosperity. For the rails did open up the vast mountain-locked valley to a flourishing commerce, just as the Denver & Rio Grande officials knew it would.

Starting in 1878, Alamosa was connected to Denver, Colorado Springs, and Pueblo by the Denver & Rio Grande Railroad. Entrance into the San Luis Valley was via 9,380 foot La Veta Pass. Passenger service between Alamosa and Denver continued until 1953. (Western History Department, Denver Public Library)

The Alamosa, a parlor-diner car made daily trips between the cities of Alamosa and Durango. The car was in service until January, 1951. (Photo by R. W. Richardson, Colorado Railroad Museum)

Tiny freight trains such as this one brought the products of the San Luis Valley and its surrounding hills into Alamosa's busy rail yards. This train is headed into the valley from Cumbres Pass. (Western History Department, Denver Public Library)

Mule Shoe Curve, a few miles below the summit of La Veta Pass. The first trains into the San Luis Valley passed over these narrow gauge rails. Later, the railroad was re-routed over a standard gauge road and this became an auto highway. (Western History Department, Denver Public Library)

During the 1920's and the 1930's, Alamosa's giant Denver & Rio Grande shops gave work to about 600 men, providing the city with a monthly payroll of some $150,000.

Turn-of-the-century Alamosa was very much a railroad town. Then, much of the city's commercial life still centered on Sixth Street. The "X" locates the Denver & Rio Grande Depot which burned in 1907. (San Luis Valley Resource Center)

As late as 1907, there were still a few rooming houses and saloons on Sixth Street between Hunt and Denver which catered to railroad men. (San Luis Valley Resource Center)

Alamosa's Chamber of Commerce office, located in pretty Cole Park, is housed in the old Narrow Gauge Museum which once stood in South Alamosa. Narrow gauge engine #169, which once pulled trains between Alamosa and Durango, is as rest there beside an 1880 car used by Denver & Rio Grande officials (Chamber of Commerce)

The Rio Grande, a hotel for railroaders. It had a pretty shady reputation during its later years. The corner part of the building, built in 1880, was the home of Alamosa's first bank. (San Luis Valley Resource Center)

The Globe Express Company.

Denver, Colorado Springs and Pueblo to Alamosa, Durango and Silverton.

Via La Veta Pass.

READ DOWN		Miles from Denver.	STATIONS. 12-10-1905	READ UP	
No. 441 No. 451. Accom. Daily	No. 115. Daily			No. 116. Daily	No. 442 No. 452 Accom. Daily
....	7 00PM	0.0	lv....Denver U. D....ar	7 30AM	....
....	9 30PM	74.9	lv. Colorado Springs .ar	4 40AM	....
....	10 45PM	119.4	ar ..Pueblo U. D. lv	3 15AM	....
....	* 11 05PM		lv ..Pueblo U. D. ar	3 00AM	....
....	11 20PM	121.4	........Minnequa........	2 40AM	....
....	....	127.8	.......San Carlos.......	....	....
....	....	145.7	........Graneros........	....	....
....	....	156.7	........Huerfano........	....	....
....	1 20AM	168.7	......Cuchara Jc't......	12 50AM	....
....	1 33AM	175.2	......Walsenburg......	11 50PM	....
....	2 40AM	190.3	........La Veta........	11 40PM	....
....	2 55AM	194.9	........Francisco........	11 22PM	....
....	3 30AM	201.9	..........Codo..........	10 50PM	....
....	4 00AM	207.2	.....La Veta Pass.....	10 25PM	....
....	4 23AM	214.6	.........Blanca.........	9 43PM	....
....	4 30AM	216.9	.........Russell.........	9 36PM	....
....	4 40AM	221.1	........Mortimer........	9 26PM	....
....	4 54AM	227.7	........Garland........	9 12PM	....
....	5 15AM	239.8	.........Baldy..........	8 52PM	....
....	5 27AM	248.3	.........Hayes.........	8 37PM	....
....	‡ 5 35AM	251.7	ar ....Alamosa..... lv	8 30PM	....
7 45PM	6 40AM		lv ....Alamosa..... ar	‡ 7 45PM	3 25PM
9 04PM	7 11AM	26 .2	........La Jara........	7 10PM	2 05PM
9 48PM	7 28AM	273.3	.........Romeo.........	6 52PM	1 35PM
10 48PM	7 45AM	280.3	ar ....Antonito.... lv	6 35PM	12 55PM
11 13PM	7 55AM		lv ....Antonito.... ar	6 27PM	12 30PM
12 17AM	8 22AM	290.7	.........Lava..........	6 01PM	11 30AM
1 16AM	8 46AM	299.4	........Bighorn........	5 38PM	10 40AM
2 10AM	9 05AM	306.1	........Sublette........	5 17PM	9 50AM
2 49AM	9 21AM	310.5	.........Toltec.........	5 02PM	9 21AM
....	9 36AM	315.3	........Toltec Gorge....	4 47PM	....
3 38AM	9 48AM	318.4	..........Osier..........	4 34PM	8 25AM
4 02AM	10 01AM	322.1	.........Los Pinos.....	4 20PM	8 05AM
5 11AM	10 25AM	330.6	.........Cumbres.......	3 55PM	7 20AM
5 50AM	10 54AM	335.5	.........Cresco.........	3 30PM	5 50AM
6 40AM	11 11AM	339.9	.........Lobato.........	3 09PM	4 45AM
7 05AM	‡ 11 25AM	344.1	ar ....Chama.... lv	2 55PM	3 55AM
8 15AM	11 45AM		lv ....Chama.... ar	‡ 2 35PM	4 45PM
8 45AM	11 58AM	349.2	......Willow Creek......	2 22PM	4 15PM
9 15AM	12 10PM	354.0	.........Azotea.........	2 09PM	3 45PM
10 18AM	12 34PM	363.5	.........Monero........	1 43PM	2 00PM
11 14AM	12 47PM	366.9	........Amargo........	1 30PM	1 30PM
11 44AM	12 54PM	369.5	......Lumberton........	1 20PM	12 54PM
12 14PM	1 09PM	373.3	........Dulce..........	1 09PM	12 15PM
12 56PM	1 21PM	377.6	........Navajo..........	12 56PM	11 45AM
1 46PM	1 46PM	386.7	........Juanita..........	12 30PM	11 00AM
2 10PM	1 55PM	390.4	....Pagosa Junction..	12 18PM	10 25AM
2 40PM	2 09PM	395.2	.......Carracas.........	12 05PM	10 00AM
3 25PM	2 31PM	403.6	.......Arboles.........	11 43AM	9 15AM
4 10PM	2 50PM	410.8	........Vallejo..........	11 24AM	8 40AM
4 50PM	3 10PM	418.9	.......La Boca.........	11 03AM	8 00AM
5 30PM	3 29PM	425.7	.......Ignacio.........	11 43AM	7 25AM
6 25PM	3 59PM	437.3	.......Florida.........	10 13AM	6 25AM
7 20PM	4 23PM	445.9	.........Bocea.........	9 48AM	5 45AM
7 55PM	4 40PM	451.5	ar......Durango......lv	* 9 30AM	5 15AM
....	* 5 00PM	451.5	lv......Durango......ar	9 15AM	....
....	7 30PM	496.7	ar.....Silverton..... lv	* 9 05AM	....

The Globe Express Company

CREEDE BRANCH.

READ DOWN No. 409. Daily	Miles	STATIONS. 12-4-1904	READ UP No. 410. Daily
7 00AM	0.0	lv.....Alamosa.....ar	‡ 7 25PM
7 25AM	10.8	........Parma.......	7 01PM
7 41AM	17.2	.....Monte Vista....	6 45PM
7 58AM	23.7	.......Haywood......	6 28PM
8 18AM	31.1	......Del Norte.....	6 07PM
8 39AM	40.2	.......Granger......	5 45PM
8 56AM	46.5	......South Fork.....	5 28PM
9 33AM	60.4	. Wagon Wheel Gap	4 50PM
9 51AM	66.4	........Wason......	4 30PM
10 00AM	68.9	ar......Creede.....lv	4 20PM

CRESTONE BRANCH.

No. 3-328 Daily Except Sun.	Miles	STATIONS. 12-10-1905	No. 330-16 Daily Except Sun.
8 00PM	0.0	Lv. Denver. Ar	7 30AM
10 35PM	74.9	" .Colo. Spgs. "	4 40AM
11 55AM	119.4	Lv. Pueblo. Ar	3 00AM
....	......	Lv. Alamosa. Ar	5 15PM
† 8 00AM	215.1	Lv. Salida. Ar	....
12 15PM	262.7	Ar. Moffat. Lv	2 05PM
12 15PM	262.7	Lv. Moffat.. Ar	2 05PM
1 00PM	273.7	Ar. Crestone. Lv	† 1 20PM

SANTA FE BRANCH.

READ DOWN No. 425 Daily Except Sun.	Miles from Denver.	STATIONS. 12-4-1904	READ UP No 426 Daily Except Sun.
8 10AM	280.3	lv....Antonito....ar	6 20PM
8 48AM	291.7	......Palmilla......	5 44PM
9 11AM	298.7	......Volcano......	5 24PM
9 39AM	307.9	......No Agua......	4 54PM
10 00AM	315.1	...Tres Piedras...	4 32PM
10 29AM	324.7	.....Servilletta.....	4 02PM
11 05AM	336.5	......Caliente......	3 26PM
11 31AM	345.1	......Barranca......	3 00PM
‡12 06PM	352.6	ar ..Embudo.. lv	2 11PM
12 26PM		lv ..Embudo.. ar	‡ 1 51PM
12 50PM	360.6	.......Alcalde.......	1 27PM
1 09PM	366.8	......Chamita.......	1 09PM
1 26PM	371.6	ar . Espanola. lv	12 51PM
1 26PM		lv . Espanola. ar	12 51PM
1 48PM	378.5	...San Ildefonso...	12 30PM
1 55PM	380.9	....Rio Grande.....	12 20PM
2 08PM	384.1	......Buckman.....	12 10PM
2 43PM	393.8	.......Jacona.......	11 40AM
3 30PM	405.3	ar...Santa Fe..lv	11 00AM

Denver & Rio Grande Railroad timetables, 1906.

Alamosa's first highway link to the east was over the old wooden state bridge. It stood in about the same spot as today's Rio Grande bridge. The arrow to the left points to the city's first important school building; the one to the right locates the Alexander Cameron Hunt house. The photo was by O. T. Davis, Alamosa's early photographer. (State Historical Society of Colorado)

FROM TOWN TO CITY

By the mid-1880's, frontier Alamosa started acting a little more like a city should. By then the Presbyterians and the Episcopalians had both moved into nice new church buildings. A new brick school house, large enough to accommodate 200 pupils, had been built out on State. It was under the direction of a Mr. E. C. Stevens, described by a writer of the time as being "a ripe scholar." A fire department had been organized; plans were under way for a new fairground to be built on the west side of town; and *The Alamosa Independent,* a weekly newspaper, kept the citizens informed. Neat cottages were springing up away from the honky-tonk business center, and Alexander Cameron Hunt and others with a little money built near-mansions facing the river and Mt. Blanca in the north part of town.

There was also considerable expansion in the business section. The banking house of Daniels, Brown & Co., established in Del Norte in 1876, moved to Alamosa in 1880 as the Bank of San Juan. It was soon afterward incorporated as the First National Bank of Alamosa, with a paid up capital of $50,000. Its first home, at the corner of Hunt and Sixth, was described as "elegant, large, well appointed, and arranged in the best possible manner for the speedy transaction of business." Wm. Sabine, a director of the bank, operated a highly respected insurance business. Alva Adams and his young brother "Billy," who were both to go far in Colorado politics, ran a massive store selling farm and mining supplies. Isaac Hill's place was even larger. He was the biggest hay and grain dealer in the valley and did a thriving business supplying the ditch companies then involved in lacing the valley together with irrigation canals. Alamosans bought their drugs and medicines from Dubendorff & Duddleston.

While there were a few new business blocks springing up around town, much of the commercial center still clustered around the old Garland City buildings, now more lopsided and weather-beaten than ever. Before 1890, there was some indication the city was going to grow away from the tracks up State and along Fifth (now Main). A Salida writer visiting Alamosa then reported:

> "The present business portion of the town runs the full length of Sixth Street where each store has a plate glass front, its awning and a spacious walk for pedestrians. But the demands of the times are calling for the further expansion of State Avenue, where it is an open secret ten 2-story buildings will be built by spring."

It was during this flurry of building activity that the Masonic Temple was built, and kitty-corner from it, the Manders Building. By then the First National Bank had moved to its new home at Fifth and San Juan. No doubt about it. Fifth Street was about to become Alamosa's "Main Street."

Alamosa's first bank, (later it became The First National Bank) stood at the corner of Sixth and Hunt. The arrow points to the second home of the First Presbyterian Church at 414 Fifth (Main). It was built in 1880 at a cost of $1500 and moved here from its first location on Ninth Street (San Luis Valley Resource Center)

One of Alamosa's first more imposing business blocks. It was located between State and San Juan on Fifth Street. "Doc" Ball, operator of the drug store, was one of the city's leading citizens. The Ball Block was completed in September, 1891. (State Historical Society of Colorado)

When Alamosa's business district centered on Sixth Street, Field & Hill and Haskins & Ball were leading suppliers of groceries and drugs. (Western History Department, Denver Public Library)

Before the water of the Rio Grande was trapped for irrigation, it was no small river. Here in this 1906 photo it is spanned by the state bridge. The arrow points to the Denver & Rio Grande Railroad's shop buildings. (Western History Department, Denver Public Library)

The home of Alexander Cameron Hunt as seen from the east bank of the Rio Grande. The house later became the home of "Doc" Ball, the druggist. It still stands at the north end of Cole Park and serves as the Alamosa Senior Citizen Center. (Western History Department, Denver Public Library)

The Alamosa Club. Built in 1891, the club boasted a reading and billard room on its first floor and a card room upstairs. During the 1930's, it housed the Cornum Hospital. In later years, before its demolition in 1973, it was a rooming house. (State Historical Society of Colorado)

An early Alamosa residence. This was the home of William Sabine, city official and banker. The house was built in 1879. (Western History Department, Denver Public Library)

A few days before Christmas, 1891, a big blaze wiped out much of ugly, old Alamosa, making way for the new. It wasn't planned that way. But a woman working at the Perry House attemped to build a fire in a stove there using kerosene. The explosion that followed tore the old frame building apart. Many neighboring buildings burned, along with the once popular hotel. Buildings not destroyed by fire were blasted away to save others. In only a few hours, a quarter of a block, where the Victoria Hotel was later built, was a field of hot ashes.

Even before the big fire, which really paved the way for a neater downtown, another giant step had been made toward making Alamosa a better place in which to live. On April 3, 1890, electric lights flashed on for the first time! On the golden anniversary of that event, the *Daily Courier* reported the occasion with this charming story:

> "A half century ago tonight a little group of Alamosans convered on a two-story house on the north side of Main street, just east of State avenue. As they walked along the boardwalks in the darkness and picked their way across the muddy intersections, furrowed by buggy wheels and horses' hoofs, they talked excitedly about what they were about to witness when they arrived at the two-story house — the home of John Spriestersbach, pioneer merchant and financier of Alamosa.
>
> "Spriestersbach himself presided over the ceremonies in his sumptuous residence. When the wondering guests had seated themselves, he stepped up to the wall and, with the air of a magician exhibiting the wonders of his profession, reached out and pressed a switch.
>
> "There were ah's and oh's as the little globes hanging from the ceiling suddenly gave forth a glow that lighted the entire room. It was a light such as those gathered there had never seen before. It gave forth no heat, but the illumination was bright and cheery. There was no flicker, no smell of kerosene, no smoking chimney."

The little 1890 light plant had a capacity of 600 electric lights and was turned off at midnight every night.

Mr. Spriesterbach, who flipped the switch that gave Alamosa lights, had come to town to be an associate of Alva Adams, who by then had left the valley for a career in politics. Spriesterbach was part of the new breed to seek a fortune in the booming city. Other businesses opening about this time included Sol Schwartz' Chicago Clothing House; Hellman & Schiffer, booksellers; John Frank & Bro., jewelry; and the city's second bank, the Bank of Alamosa. By this time, too, "Doc" Ball had established his popular drug store, stocking among other things according to an early ad, "— the best of wines and liquors for medicinal purposes." The city had several doctors and one dentist.

There were new churches too. The Catholics and the Methodists had come to town. Some sixty Masons were meeting in the new temple, and the Odd Fellows Lodge had been established with forty members meeting in the Manders Building. The valley's most exclusive club, The Alamosa, had been established and moved into its posh new Main Street home. Slavick's, an elegant and respectable place, opened over on Sixth Street's "saloon row."

Another fire, soon after the turn of the century, changed the looks of Alamosa again. On Christmas Day, 1907, the big yellow Denver & Rio Grande depot burned to the ground. While the handsome new brick building, which still stands, was under construction, the railroad improvised a makeshift depot out of two old box cars and one passenger coach. A ridiculous looking thing, it became known as "Noah's Ark."

By the turn of the century, Alamosa's population had passed the 1000 mark. Compared to the town that had been hauled in and set up on the river banks twenty-two years earlier, it was beginning to look pretty good. But Alamosa still had a lot of growing up to do. That would come as the San Luis Valley's fertile, irrigated fields started to blossom to create a new and healthy economy.

The First National Bank. One of Alamosa's first brick buildings, it was at the corner of Sixth & Hunt. Later the building, which still stands, housed the Rio Grande Hotel.

The Masonic Hall, built in 1887, has been an imposing Alamosa landmark for almost ninety years. It was the first major building to be constructed on what would become Alamosa's Main Street. (San Luis Valley Resource Center)

The Manders Building. It was constructed in 1891 at the corner of Main and San Juan when Alamosa started to grow away from the railroad. (Western History Department, Denver Public Library)

The first home of the First National Bank at its Main and San Juan location. (San Luis Valley Resource Center)

The First Presbyterian Church, built in 1896. It stood at the corner of Fourth and San Juan. (San Luis Valley Resource Center)

The Victoria, built in 1901, on the site of the old Perry House was Alamosa's most popular hotel for over half a century. John D. Rockefeller and William Jennings Bryan stopped there. Every passenger train arriving in Alamosa was met by one of "The Vic's" uniformed black porters. (Photo by Sandra Dallas, Western History Department, Denver Public Library)

State Street, looking south during the early 1920's. The flag is flying from the Elks Club Building. Then the post office was located there. The Carnegie Library, across the street, opened in 1910 with 1500 books. Next to it is the First Baptist Church, built in 1907. Alamosa's street lights then stood right in the middle of the street.

Horse and buggy days are about over. The view is north on State, with the depot to the right and the Victoria Hotel to the left.

Turn-of-the-century Alamosa. Originally named Fifth, the city's main street was by then being called Main. Starting in the mid-1880's businesses began the move away from the depot, up State, and spilled around the corner to form what would be the San Luis Valley's commercial center. (State Historical Society of Colorado)

Not yet paved, new sidewalks are being built along Main Street during the early 1920's. Then street lamps stood in the middle of Main and that is where shoppers parked their cars. The Alamosa National Bank faces Main at the corner of State. (Western History Department, Denver Public Library.)

With street lamps, electric signs, automobiles and brand new sidewalks, Alamosa began to look like a city during the 1920's. The handsome building in the center of the block housed the Isis Theatre. Later, Everett Cole turned it into the Coconut Grove Ballroom, and then, the Grove Theatre. (Western History Department, Denver Public Library)

Labor Day, 1911. People from all over the San Luis Valley stand along a decorated State Street to see the mile long parade. Later, they gathered at the Alamosa Fairgrounds for races and baseball. (San Luis Valley Resource Center)

The American Legion Building under construction. The cornerstone was laid in 1924 by United States Vice President Dawes. The building now houses the popular Rialto Theatre.

A far cry from Alamosa's modern 100-bed hospital, this was the medical center of the San Luis Valley during the early part of the century. A handsome building, it still stands at the corner of Hunt and Main.

One of the artesian wells of the Alamosa Water Works. Drilled in 1911, it was 863 feet deep and produced 13,320 gallons of water each hour.

The valley's communication center during the early part of the century.

Alamosa's largest church, Sacred Heart. It was built at a cost of $100,000 in 1927.

After Nathan's moved out of this State and Main landmark, the popular Herrick & Olson moved in. Later it was the home of the Sherman Drug Co.

A NEW KIND OF ECONOMY

Alamosa's continuing growth, during the early part of the new century, hinged directly on the San Luis Valley's farm and ranch economy. Even the city's few industries were linked to the land. The railroad became more and more dependent on farm and ranch shipments for its income.

The valley's level land was exceedingly rich. But being more or less an arid country, it needed water to be productive. The first Spanish-speaking colonists who came into the San Luis area from northern New Mexico brought with them a few head of livestock, some seeds, and the knowledge of irrigation. Between 1852, when they dug the People's Ditch, and 100 years later when the Platoro Dam was completed, the people of the valley trapped almost every stream for later use on the rich farm fields. When the land and water got together under the valley's bright sun and crisp nights, incredible yields were assured.

This mass of farm produce found its way to markets in the East by way of Alamosa. During one year alone, 1930, a year of country-wide depression, 11,000 carloads of potatoes were shipped from the San Luis Valley. "Spuds" were the big cash crop. But that same year, over 2,200 carloads of vegetables were pulled out of the valley over the Denver & Rio Grande's tracks. Of these, 700 cars were full of head lettuce. Others were packed with peas, cauliflower, broccoli, cabbage, and spinach. Much of the choice produce was grown by industrious Japanese farmers.

The livestock business was big, too. Alamosa's stockyards, during the early part of the century, handled more animals than any yard in southern Colorado. During 1930, 780 carloads of cattle passed through the Alamosa yards. Over 900 carloads of sheep went to market via Alamosa. And 110 carloads of hogs were shipped out of Alamosa. The hogs were fattened on peas right in the field, and there was much talk in the valley then about "Peas, Pigs and Prosperity!"

Long before the growing of livestock became big business in the valley, its fertile fields produced grain crops of exceptional quality. Even before the turn of the century, the Alamosa Milling & Elevator Company, using valley grown wheat, was turning out some 300 barrels of Blanca and Four Aces Flour every day for the Colorado and Southwest market. Since the 1930's barley has been a big crop in the valley, with Coors buying much of it for the beer they brew in Golden.

As the giant shops of the Denver & Rio Grande were expanded in Denver, as the equipment became more sophisticated, and as more and more trucks were seen on the valley's farm roads, the payroll at Alamosa's shops began to slip. In ten years time, the number of men on the staff there dropped from 600 to about a third that many. One time railroaders and newcomers to the city found jobs in the few industries scattered around town.

There was the already mentioned Alamosa Milling and Elevator Company. K & B, the valley's only meat packing house, employed several men. So did the Alamosa Creamery, whose ice cream, butter and cheese were sold in three states. One of the larger employers was Railways Ice Company. Its $250,000 plant, east of town, produced the vast amount of ice required each year to pack the valley's fresh vegetable shipments. The Public Service power plant employed a fair number of people and so did the little 1000-barrels-a-day Oriental Refining Company whose raw product was trucked into the city from Pagosa Springs. The city, as it had been from the start, continued to be a distribution center and several big wholesale houses were located there.

Early in its life, Alamosa became the largest and most important town in Conejos County. But it was not until 1913, under a bill introduced by the then State Senator "Billy" Adams, that Alamosa County came into being. Carved out of parts of Conejos and Costilla Counties, Alamosa was the last county to be established in Colorado. Alamosa, with a population of just over 3,000 was made county seat. Because the new county inherited a large debt from Conejos County, it could not afford a real court house until 1938. Then one was built with W.P.A. help.

The county provided the city with its first important government payroll. Later, with the payrolls of Adams State and other local, state, and federal agencies, government would be the city's biggest employer.

The handsome Alamosa County courthouse was built in 1938.

Established in 1890, the Alamosa Milling and Elevator Company produced some 300 barrels of flour daily for Colorado markets. Over 100,000 bushels of valley grown wheat could be stored in the huge elevator. (Western History Department, Denver Public Library)

The city's early industries, such as the Alamosa Packing Company, were related to the valley's farm and ranch economy. During the early years, the Rio Grande splashed out of its banks about every spring flooding much of Alamosa. (San Luis Valley Resource Center)

During the 1950's, Alamosa County ranked 47th in the nation in potato production. This harvest scene was taken on the William Martin Ranch. (San Luis Valley Resource Center)

While several kinds of potatoes have been grown in the San Luis Valley over the years, it is best known for the Red McClure. Yields of up to 450 bushels are common.

Sales every Saturday at Hank Wiescamp's Alamosa Auction. It has been a South Alamosa landmark and livestock exchange center for well over a third of a century. (Chamber of Commerce)

During the 1930's, over 700 carloads of head lettuce were shipped each year to Eastern markets from the San Luis Valley's fertile fields. Many of the field workers migrated to the valley each harvest season from California, Arizona, and Texas.

MR. ALAMOSA — William H. "Billy" Adams. Three term governor of Colorado, Adams devoted over fifty years of his life to quality public service. Adams State College, named for him, was his proudest achievement. In 1953, at 92, Adams, who had only a grammar school education, was given a Degree of Doctor of Humanities and Public Service by the college he founded.

BILLY ADAMS AND HIS COLLEGE

The first thought of a college to be located in Alamosa grew out of the mind of William H. "Billy" Adams, pioneer San Luis Valley cattle rancher, who gave over fifty years of his life to public service. He was Colorado's governor for three terms during the 1920's. He served ten terms in the state senate — one in the house of representatives. Earlier, Adams had been an Alamosa County Commissioner, and twice he was Alamosa's mayor. The accomplishments of this gentle, quiet man were many, but the one of which he was most proud was the establishment of Adams State College, something he had on his mind since 1890.

In 1921, under the continuing pressure of the then politically strong Adams, the twenty-third General Assembly authorized a school to be called the State Normal School at Alamosa. Two years later, the twenty-fourth General Assembly appropriated $75,000 for its first building and gave the name Adams State Normal School to the budding college. On August 31, 1923, the cornerstone of the building was laid. That first building, now the central part of the administration building, was completed in 1924. That same year, Ira Richardson was named the college's first president.

In September of 1925, after a well attended summer session, forty-two students enrolled for the first regular school year. The faculty numbered three, including President Richardson, Elizabeth Briggs, and Tessie Degan.

The Adams State Normal School offered diplomas, then carrying life authority to teach in the schools of Colorado at the end of an accepted two or four year course of study. Students paid a fee of $8.00 per quarter plus a "student relationship" fee of not more than $4.00 per quarter on registering. Board costs varied from $5.00 to $7.00 per week, and rooms rented for $12.00 to $15.00 a month.

Though the struggles were many during President Richardson's twenty-five year reign, so were the accomplishments. Adams State was unknown when he arrived in Alamosa to head it up. A quarter of a century later, it was an accredited school with a fine national reputation. Under Richardson's devoted direction, he saw Adams State grow from one little brick building in the middle of a sage brush patch to a beautifully landscaped campus of handsome halls and dormitories. It was no small job. But in spite of a major depression and World War II, Richardson still managed to pull the whole thing together. Only a man with his kind of concern for the individual could have done it.

After Richardson's resignation in 1950, Dr. N. William Newsom assumed the presidency for two years. Then Luther Bean, pioneer Adams State educator, stepped in as acting president for two months. On June 3, 1952, Dr. Fred J. Plachy came on the scene, and Adams State took off like a rocket! The student body numbered 359 when this man of unbounded energy took command. Fourteen years later, when he retired to be replaced by Dr. John A. Marvel, there were 2,310 students on campus.

By 1975, when Adams State College celebrated its fiftieth birthday, it had granted degrees to more than 9,000 persons. By then 2,800 students were on the 100 acre campus. Almost 300 persons were on the college staff. The annual budget was $7,580,000. "Billy" Adams' college was a rip-roaring success!

Most of Alamosa turned out on August 31, 1923 to see the cornerstone laid for the new Normal School. The Masonic Lodge conducted the ceremony. (Adams State College)

Adams State's first building, now the central part of Richardson hall, was completed in 1924. (Adams State College)

Ira Richardson, Adams State's president from 1924 until 1950. His deep concern for the individual made "Prexie" a very special person to all those who were on campus during his administration. (Adams State College)

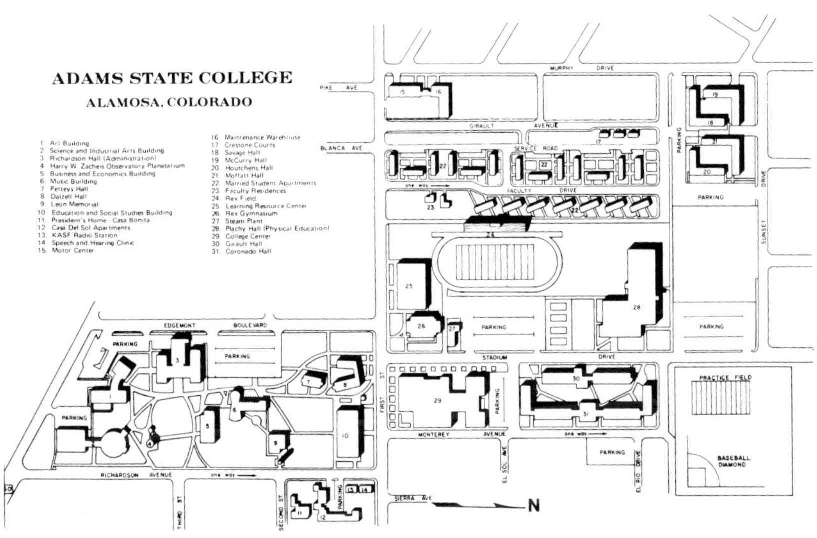

Adams State, a liberal arts college offering both graduate and undergraduate degrees, now sprawls over ninety acres with an enrollment of almost 3,000; 300 are on the college payroll. (Adams State College)

Alamosa High School destroyed by fire in April, 1930, was replaced immediately by a larger, better building. Now, it serves as Alamosa Junior High.

Until it was brought under control, the Rio Grande splashed over its banks almost every spring. Here, West Main Street is under water. At the other end of Main Street, where the red light district was located, "the girls were packed out piggy-back, darn near every spring" according to a long time Alamosa marshal. (San Luis Valley Resource Center)

DEPRESSION DAYS

With 100 pound sacks of potatoes selling for as little as 35c, and other farm and ranch prices being equally low, not very much money circulated in the San Luis Valley's big city during the late 1920's and early 1930's. It was a gloomy time. Except for Saturday traffic, encouraged by all sorts of city-widè promotions, Alamosa's streets were very quiet.

It was a time, however, when a dollar bought a lot. Meals at the Grand and other Alamosa restaurants could be had for as little as 35c. Safeway sold bacon for 27c a pound and two pounds of lunch meat for 25c. Daniel's and Kelloff's food stores priced coffee at 27c a pound. Twenty-three cents bought three pounds of flour, and 25c was the price for a pound of butter. Ice cream sodas at the Valley Cut Rate's fountain were a nickle. Gordon's advertised ladies' frocks for 98c and men's coats for $2.98. A new Dodge sedan could be bought at Mc Dermith's for $815.00. The city's only parking lot charged 15c a day. Ward's sold motor oil for 12c a quart, and Kirkpatrick's priced nifty two-piece velour living rooms sets at $59.00. A movie ticket could be purchased for as little as a dime, with the chance of winning a "Bank-Night" cash prize.

When the harvest season rolled around, there were a few jobs to be had in the farm fields and in the packing sheds. The Denver & Rio Grande's payroll climbed up a little. This gave Alamosa's summer economy some lift. But when that short season ended, the valley was again filled with people who simply could not find work.

Some of the more ambitious young people took advantage of these hard times to begin their education at Adams State. This posed a serious problem for President Richardson, as they arrived without money for tuition, room and board, and he didn't know how to turn them away. Leaving the campus, Richardson scrounged around town looking for work for his would-be students. Many young men ended up in Alamosa basements stoking furnaces in exchange for a place to sleep and a meal a day. Girls, too, traded their help for board and room. Part-time jobs in town and on campus helped pay the modest tuition costs.

As the country was starting to emerge from the depression, radio station KGIW went on the air knitting the valley's far-flung people into sort of a family. The station's voice was heard first in September of 1933. Established by Gus Jenkins, it was soon sold to Will Thomas. During the mid-1930's, under the colorful management of Don Bennett, KGIW's programming was highly innovative.

Another 1930's innovation was the Alarado Celebration. A three day affair, which always included the 4th of July, it combined parades and baseball games with an air circus and rodeo. But the really big show was the outdoor extravaganza staged at Adams State's athletic field after dark. Huge casts in beautiful costumes, backed with full orchestras, were featured in ambitions productions relating to the valley's colorful history. Even though the Alarado was enthusiastically produced and promoted, it never picked up enough momentum to carry it on but a few years.

Then Alamosans had to settle for less sophisticated entertainments, such as Billie Bates dance recitals (admission 10c). There were also piano recitals by Evelyn Tozier's students, and an occasional concert by the little, but spirited, Alamosa Philharmonic Orchestra. Each Christmas, Alamosa became one of the most beautifully decorated little cities in Colorado, largely through the efforts of Carl Johnson of the Public Service Company.

By 1937 Alamosa was well on its way up from the trying times that had slowed its growth. That year a record $440,000 was spent on buildings, in cluding the new Alamosa County Court House, a hospital, state highway building, and Daniel's new supermarket.

Once again, "Moosie,"(as it was called by some), was on the move! With a population of 5,000, it was, by all odds, the valley's largest and most important city.

The Rialto, showplace of the San Luis Valley. From 1937 until his death in 1974, Joe Brite dazzled Alamosa theatre-goers daily with his performances at the giant Wurlitzer.

Looking down on Alamosa in the mid-1940's. The numbers locate a dozen of the city's landmark buildings. 1. Sacred Heart Church. 2. Post Office. 3. First Presbyterian Church. 4. Methodist Church of Seven Gables. 5. Alamosa County Court House. 6. Elk's Club. 7. Mander Block. 8. Masonic Temple. 9. Walsh Hotel, the valley's favorite eating place for generations. 10. Victoria Hotel. 11. Depot. 12. Columbia Hall, meeting place of the S.P.M.D.T.U. Spanish-American organization.

Alamosa was air-linked to the outside world for the first time in November of 1946 when Monarch Air Lines, (Frontier Air Lines predecessor company) started daily flights through the San Luis Valley from Denver to Durango and return. The little DC-3 "gooneybirds" stopped twice daily in Alamosa. (Frontier Air Lines photo)

Fort Garland today. It was built in 1858 and maintained until 1883. More a refuge and social center for early San Luis Valley settlers than a military post, it was once commanded by Kit Carson.

The site of Pike's Stockade, near Sanford is now a National Historical Landmark. Zebulon Pike and his Company spent the winter of 1806-1807 here.

THE SUMMER INVASION

When summer came, after the depression was over, and people from Texas, Kansas, Oklahoma, and other hot-weather states took to the road looking for a place to cool off and play, Alamosa began to harvest a new kind of crop. The Chamber of Commerce hammered away with a campaign to lure people to the Valley using the theme — "You haven't seen Colorado if you haven't seen the San Luis Valley!" It worked. The tourists, bless 'em, poured through the city on their way to the many attractions that surrounded it.

For ninety days or so each year, the hotels, cottage camps, and restaurants did a brisk business. Sam Gardenswartz sold the visitors fly rods, flies, and shotgun shells. Daniels and all the other grocery stores in town sent the tourists on their way with their trunks full of camping supplies. Gasoline and tire sales zoomed at the city's filling stations. Being the valley's natural gateway city, Alamosa caught the tourists coming and going, and the trickle of new dollars they left behind was vital to the economy.

Most Valley visitors came for the superb trout fishing and to hunt for duck, elk, and deer. Many more came just to ogle the magnificent scenery in the San Juan and Sangre de Cristo Mountains. All were charmed with the mining towns of Bonanza, Crestone, Summitville, Platoro, and especially Creede. They were fascinated by the quaint old Spanish villages of Conejos and San Luis, oldest settlements in Colorado and with the early Mormon communities of Manassa, Sanford, and Richfield. History buffs explored Fort Garland, once commanded by Kit Carson, and Pike's Stockade, where the famed explorer, Zebulon Pike, spent the winter of 1806-1807. They enjoyed the dude ranches up Rio Grande and Conejos Canyons. They were fascinated by the artesian wells, numerous hot springs, 200 acre fields of potatoes, and the neat Japanese truck farms. They rode the narrow gauge trains, went to rodeos, and raved about the blue sky and near-perfect climate. But the valley's biggest sight was the Sand Dunes.

Established in 1932 as a national monument by President Hoover, the Great Sand Dunes covers an area of about fifty-seven square miles at the foot of the Sangre de Cristo Mountains some thirty-five miles north of Alamosa. An awesome and beautiful sight, they became known throughout the country in 1942 when "The Singing Sands of Alamosa" made the Hit Parade.

As the word spread concerning the valley's many attractions, more and more flatlanders came causing a flurry of building booms. New tourist courts sprouted up at the east and west ends of town to accommodate families fleeing the mid-west's heat. Then after World War II, with the building of the Narrow Gauge Motel and the expansion of the Walsh Hotel, Alamosa's growth as a tourist center began in earnest.

Great Sand Dunes National Monument, near Alamosa is 57 square miles of sparkling white sand cradled in the arms of the spectacular Sangre de Cristo (Blood of Christ) Mountains. Wind-sculptured dunes rise to 600 feet.

No longer a national monument as it was early in the century, Wheeler remains one of the most awesome sights in the San Juan's. It is near Creede.

State Street, 1953.

Main Street, 1953. (San Luis Valley Resource Center)

1976

If Alamosa's founding fathers were to return to the city today, they would surely be surprised and pleased. Almost a century old now, their jerry-built town has blossomed into a thoroughly modern little city offering nearly all the advantages of urban life in a still lovely and unspoiled setting.

While Alamosa's growth has never been spectacular, some 7,000 people do live there now. Another 5,000 people live in Alamosa County. Being the trade center for the San Luis Valley's 40,000 population, Alamosa looks like a much bigger city than it really is.

About one-third of the city's population is Spanish-speaking, with a sprinkling of blacks, Indians, and Orientals. This interesting mixture of people, living together in a somewhat isolated "on-top-of-the-world" spot, has developed a city with a rare kind of spirit and independence.

Proud of its past, pleased with the present, Alamosa seems ready to launch into its second century with a great deal of confidence and enthusiasm.

BIBLIOGRAPHY

BOOKS

Anderson, George, *Gen. William Jackson Palmer,* Colorado College, 1936
Athearn, Robert G., *Rebel of the Rockies,* Yale University Press, 1962
Bean, Luther, *Land of the Blue Sky People,* 1962
Beebe & Clegg, *Rio Grande, Rebel in the Rockies,* Howell-North, 1962
Griswold, Don & Jean, *Colorado's Century of Cities,* 1958
Ingersoll, Ernest, *The Crest of the Continent,* R. R. Donnelly, 1885
McAdow, Beryl, *Land of Adoption,* Johnson Publishing Co., 1970
McAdow, Beryl, *From Crested Peaks,* Big Mountain Press, 1961
Folks and Fortunes, Monte Vista Journal, 1949
Oehlerts, Donald E., *Guide to Colorado Newspapers 1859-1963,* 1964
Ormes, Robert, *Tracking Ghost Railroads in Colorado,* Century One Press, 1975
Pelton, A. R., *San Luis Valley,* Denver Art Printers, 1891
Spencer, Frank C., *The Story of the San Luis Valley,* SLV Historical Society, 1975

PAMPHLETS AND ARTICLES

Adams State College, *The First Half Century,* 1975
Clausen, Henry, *Garland City,* Denver Westerners Round Up, Vol XXIX, 7
Choda, Kelly, *Thirty Pound Rails,* Filter Press, 1965
Hester, Harriet D., *Scrapbooks, 1921-1940*
Lipsey, Julia, *Gov. Hunt of the Colorado Territory,* Western Books, 1960
McDermith, Genevieve, *Colorado's Cowboy Governor,* Pioneers of the San Juan, 1952
Leading Industries of the West, H. S. Reed & Co., 1884
Denver & Rio Grande Official Guide, Western Publishing, 1879
Slopes of the Sangre de Cristo, Denver & Rio Grande, 1898
The Great San Luis Valley, Hoeckel & Co.

UN-PUBLISHED MATERIAL

Lantis, David, *The San Luis Valley, Colorado,* Doctoral Thesis, University of Ohio, 1953

NEWSPAPERS

Alamosa Journal
Alamosa Courier
Alamosa News
Southern Coloradoan
The Denver Post
Rocky Mountain News